The seven-digit alphanumeric (e.g., GDFK-YBT for L.B.) is as unique identifier for each person listed in this volume, as recorded at familysearch.org. This is the largest free genealogy site available. You can sign up for a free account there. I can be found at LVSV-N4T

William Harold "Bill" Meadows Sr.	Rev. Linville Barton Meadors Sr.	William Bluford Meadors
1926-1964 • LTB1-MB9	1895-1980 • GDFK-YBT	1863-1934 • LYHP-K9W
Marriage: 9 July 1946	Marriage: 2 January 1922	Marriage: 10 September 1881
Catoosa, Georgia, United States	Winchester, Clark, Kentucky, United State	Whitley, Kentucky, United States
Aline Harriett Cole	Harriet Hatcher	Lucinda C Parker
1924-2006 • LTB1-QCW	1903-1995 • LTB1-QC2	1865-1898 • 2W31-J8B

The Meadows Farmily Heritage, Volume One
copyright Linville M. Meadows 2025
Published by the The Meadows Farm, Inc.
Willis, Virginia
Cover photo: my father William Harold Meadows, Sr, driving a 1920's Model T Ford with me in his lap.

ISBN 978-1-73-502588-9   51299

The Meadows Family Heritage

Volume One
Ten Generations from Prato to Meadors
1612-1980

Compiled September 2025

Linville M. Meadows

TABLE OF CONTENTS

Family Crest   6

De Prato to Meadors   7

Linville Barton Meadows, Sr. and Harriett Green Hatcher   10

William Bluford Meadors and Lucinda C. Parker   37

John W. Meadors and Mary Surrelda "Polly" White   44

Slavery in Kentucky   46

William Troy Meadors and Sarah Sally "Sarry" Smith   48

Thomas Jefferson Meadors, Jr. and Elizabeth "Betsy" Martin   50

Thomas Meador Sr., and Keziah Moberly   52

Jason Meadors, Sr. and Elizabeth Harrison Stone   58

John Meadors and Elizabeth Ann White   62

Advancement of Slavery in Virginia   65

Thomas Meador Jr. and Sarah Hoskins   66

Thomas Meade, Sr. and Sarah Yates   69

Indigenous Peoples in the Virgina Colony   73

Family Crest

Originated at Wyntesham, Suffolk County, England in 1188. It consists of a sable (black) shield with an azure (blue) chevron. The shield is divided into three sections. On two of these is a pelican plucking its breast with its beak, leaving a gules (red) spot of blood. This is a symbol of self-sacrifice, arising from a myth that pelicans wounded themselves to feed their young in times of famine. On the third section of the shield is a statant (standing) lion, a peaceful but wary stance symbolizing the guarding of home and country. The motto below the shield, Meados virtus, translates as, "My gift is virtue."

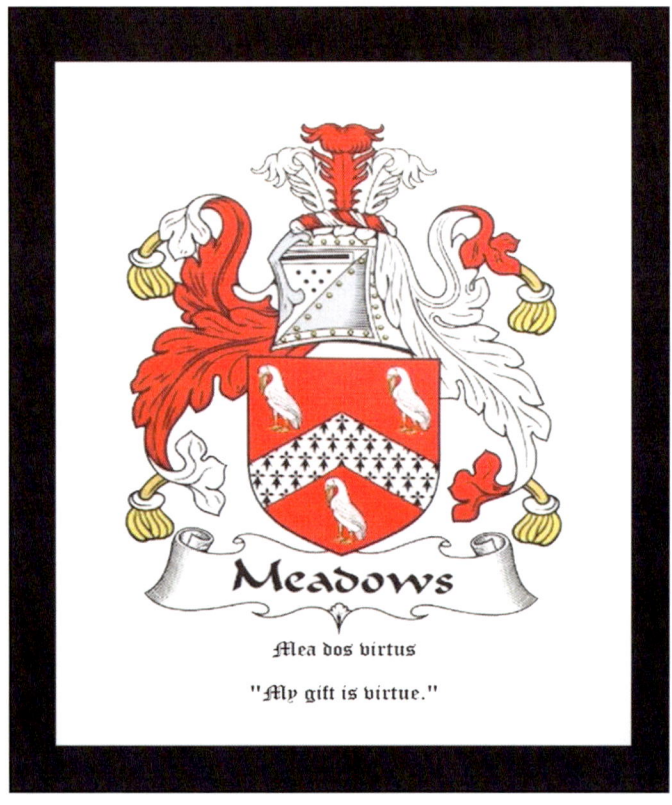

Another version is described as sable, a chevron or, between three pelicans, vulned of the last. The crest, an eagle, displayed, beaked and armed, bearing the motto: "Toujour Pret," or always ready. The eagle in the crest was given to Sir Robert Meade for his service in the cause of the German Empire in the wars of Gustavus Adolphus.

De Prato to Meadors

A History of the Meades

The name Meadows probably arose from the Norman "de Prato." Translated into the English, the name becomes Mead (and as many as 27 other spellings, including Meade, Mede, Meads; Meather, Meathes, Meador and Meadows). The name derives from the Latin pratum, a meadow; and in Old French prat, a meadow. Prat, in Dutch, signifies proud, arrogant, cunning.

1066
Norman Invasion. Presumably the name Prat and Meade crossed the English Chanel with the Normans, for there is no mention of either name in England prior to 1066.

1086
The name Witnesham appears in the Domesday Book.

1090
Edmund de Wyntesham born in Witnesham, lived in Suffolk during the latter part of the reign of William the Conqueror. The earliest known Meades ancestor, he was born in Witnesham around 1090. His descendants include a Robert de Medew (born c. 1140) and Robert Earl de Meadwe (born c. 1290), both in Suffolk. The Meade's lived in Wyntesham Hall until at least 1750.

Wyntesham Hall as it appears today

Wyntesham was described as a small struggling village and parish, containing 575 souls and 1906 acres of land, belonging to the Meadows family and a few smaller proprietors. Because of natural barriers between it and the rest of England, East Anglia had tended to be rather isolationistic. It was also noted for its outspoken political and religious non-conformists.

> **De Medewe, of Witnesham Hall, co. Suffolk.**
>
> PETER DE MEDEWE was seized of lands at Witnesham, in the 34 Henry II. (1188), and those lands have ever since remained in the family, and are now in the possession of the present representative DANIEL CHARLES DE MEDEWE, ESQ. of Witnesham Hall and Great Bealings, co. Suffolk, eldest surviving son and heir of the late Rev. Philip Meadows, Rector of Great Bealings, by Elizabeth his wife, dau. of the Rev. Morgan Graves, M.A., Rector of Redgrave cum Botesdale, and of Hinderclay, in the same county. The younger branch of the Meadows family is represented by Earl Manvers, of Thoresby Park, Notts., great-grandson of Sir Philip Meadows, Knight-Marshal of the King's Palace.
>
> **Arms.**—Gu. a chev. erm. between three pelicans, vulned, ppr.; in a canton a lion sejant, and in chief a label of three points, quartering Brewster, of Wrentham Hall, co. Suffolk, sa. a chev. erm. between three estoiles arg.
> **Crest.**—A pelican, vulned, ppr.
> **Motto.**—Mea dos virtus.

Description of Wyntesham Hall and the Coat of Arms

1180

In 1180, Norman documents record the names of William, Robert, Matilda, Roger, and Reginald de Prato; and in 1198, the names of Richard and Robert de Prato. In 1199, in Essex England (adjacent to Suffolk County) is found the name of Roger de Prato and Walter de Prato.

1200

Hervey de Prato, dubbed the "faithful knight" of King John II, was given Rouen Castle for his meritorious service. In the earliest writs of Parliament and the Hundred Rolls, in the time of King John, we find John-atte-Meadow, William-atte-Meadow and William-de-Medward, meaning John or William at the Meadow and William of the Meadows.

1280

Early records describe Henry de la Medewe in Worcestershire in 1280 AD, and Richard atte Medeue in Sussex in 1327 AD and Richard atte Medeue in Sussex in 1327. I cannot today draw a direct link from the Meades of Wyntesham and Thomas Meade Sr. I believe I have the link to Ambrose, his brother.

1569

The name Mead is recorded in the English College of Heraldry. The founder of the English branch was granted his own coat of arms.

1583

Ambrose Meador was born in Avon, Wiltshire. He migrated to the Virginia Colony in 1636, on the same ship as Thomas Meade, The Elder, and theysettled a few miles apart. I cannot as of this date, find a direct link from Thomas, the elder's father, Willliam, the the Wytnesham branch, but clearly Ambrose and his brother Thomas both immigrated to British Colonial America on the same ship and settled within a few miles of each other.

Linville Barton Meadows, Sr.

Harriet Green Hatcher

William Harold "Bill" Meadows Sr.
1926–1964 • LTB1-MB9
Marriage: 9 July 1946
Catoosa, Georgia, United States
Aline Harriett Cole
1924–2006 • LTB1-QCW

Rev. Linville Barton Meadors Sr.
1895–1980 • GDFK-YBT
Marriage: 2 January 1922
Winchester, Clark, Kentucky, United State
Harriet Hatcher
1903–1995 • LTB1-QC2

William Bluford Meadors
1863–1934 • LYHP-K9W
Marriage: 10 September 1881
Whitley, Kentucky, United States
Lucinda C Parker
1865–1898 • 2W31-J8B

Photographs of Linville Barton Meadors as a young man.

Known as L.B. as an adult, Linville Barton Sr., was born April 2, 1895 in Whitley County, Kentucky. He received only a minimal grade school education, probably to the 3rd or 5th grade. In 1908, aged 13, he got a job with the L&N Railroad making $1.26 a day. In 1920, he was promoted to brakeman. He was subsequently laid off for health reasons, cause unknown.

Brakemen were responsible for applying and releasing the train's brakes, served as a vital communication link, using hand signals or lanterns to relay instructions and information to the engineer and other crew members. They operated track switches to route trains and cars as required. Before a train's departure, they would inspect the train's length, checking couplings, air hoses, and journal boxes to ensure everything was secure and in working order. As the train's captain, the conductor oversaw the entire operation, and the brakeman would assist the conductor with various tasks, which might include checking and recording car numbers, loading and unloading cargo, and even helping passengers on and off the train.
The brakeman in the photo is not LB.

A brakeman on the L&N circa 1910

Whitley County is just north of Tennessee, due north from Knoxville. It is located within the Cumberland Plateau of southeastern Kentucky, which is greatly overlapped by the broad Eastern Coal Field region of the state. A large number of the Meadors family lived and worked there.

On January 3rd 1922, L.B. married Harriett Greene Hatcher.
She was born in July 17th, 1903 in Greensburg, Clark County, KY.
She worked as a telephone operator and was 19 when they
married; he was 27.

The Meadors lived in Whitley County, Kentucky, in Harlan, Kentucky for a short time, and in Knoxville, Tennessee. They moved to Jacksonville, Florida later in life. They had eight surviving children and many grandchildren.

Unkown woman, Harriet with William on her lap; Linville Barton holding L.B. Jr., and Irene standing; unknown female

Irene, William, Linville Jr., Linville Sr.

Irene, Ruth, William, and Harriet

Shirley, Betty, Jean, Naomi, Ruth, William, Linville Jr., Irene, Harriet, and Linville, Sr.

Linville Sr., William, Aline, Naomi, Jean, Paul, Harriet, Irene, Betty

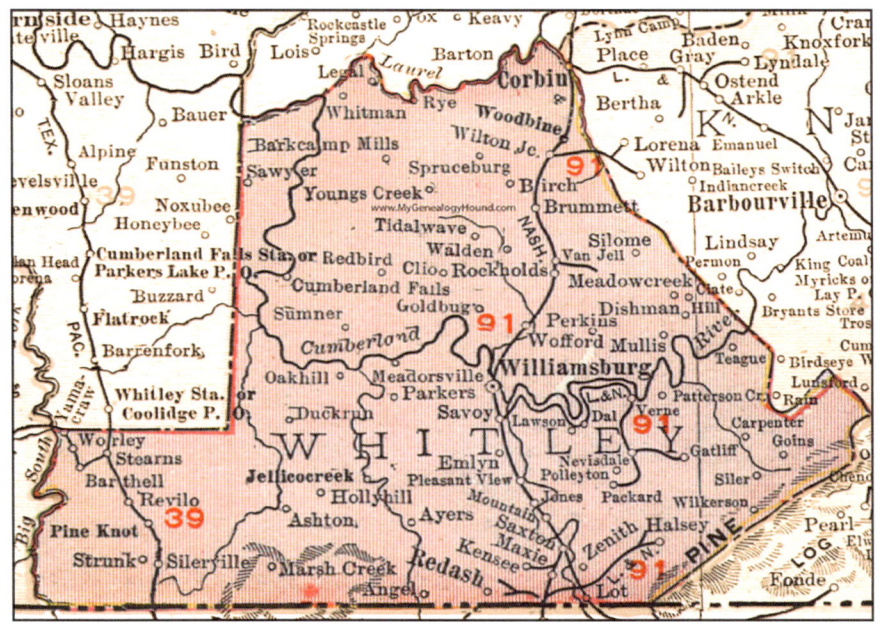

Map of Whitley County Kentucky

Naomi and Jean

Irene, Ruth, Naomi, William, Linville Jr.,

Irene, Linville Jr., Linville Sr., William

Harriet Green Hatcher

born July 7, 1903 Greensburg, Kentucky
died February 21, 1995 Maryille, Tennessee

Most genealogical records follow the male line, so information on Harriet's life is sparse. However, her importance here is her ancestors, who turn out to be important personsages in history, as we shall see. All photos on this page are of Harriet.

The Reverend L.B. Meadors

In May of 1920, L.B. was employed by Continental Casualty of Chicago. He was let go, allegedly because of his preaching.

About this time, he was employed by the Singer Sewing Machine Co. I am told he would put the sewing machine on his back and carry it up the mountain to sell.

In 1924, he professed as a Christian and joined the church. He received the call to preach in 1926 and was ordained in August 1928.

He was a self-described Baptist Evangelist, "preaching the plain old attractive Gospel exclusively."

A poster advertising Linville's On Air Broadcast on radio station WIBK

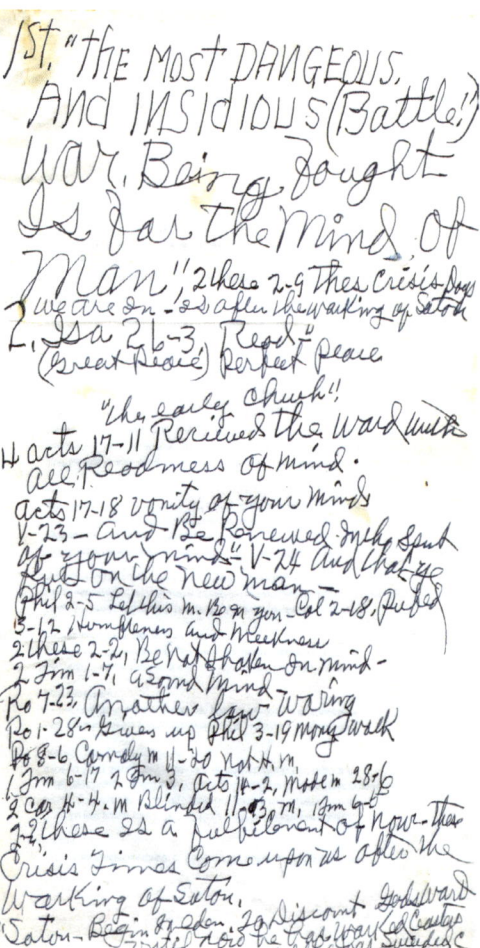

A sample of sermon notes in Linville's handwriting.

L.B. continued his ministry for the rest of his life, preaching at tent meetings, revivals and on the radio. In the traditional style, he would baptise his flock in the river. Daughters Naomi and Jean would sing and accompany him on piano.

Preaching on WNOX radio

Daughters Naomi and Jean playing piano and signing hymns

A poster announcing a sermon on the steps of the Courthouse from loudspeakers on the roof of his car.

Linville baptising his flock in the river.

A photo of Linville posing in front of an American flag.
Date unkown.

The Right Honorable Reverend Linville Barton Meadors

Not content with his Baptist Ministry, L.B. ran successfully for County Clerk of Whitley County in 1929, was elected as a representative from the 82nd District to the General Assembly in 1933, and County Judge in 1937. His tenure as County Judge was fraught with some difficulties, as we shall see.

Kentucky Assembly Building

STOP!

REV. L. B. Meadors

May this message cause you to think serious. Your friend is calling for help. He is asking for the office of County Court Clerk of Whitley County. Primary election Aug. 3, 1929 He has a wife and 4 children to support, he will endeavor to be a servant of the people in the future as in the past. He has the good people back of him in this race to depend on.

REPUBLICAN

THE PEOPLE'S CANDIDATE

L. B. MEADORS For Clerk

Promotional Material from Linville's campaign for Clerk of Court and a newspaper article he wrote as well.

Rev. L. B. Meadors

As I will not be able to see each voter personally in the interest of my campaign for County Court Clerk of Whitley County, due to a nervous breakdown 10 weeks ago in the pulpit West of Corbin. That has made me unable for manuel labor and also I am not able to be on my feet and legs long at a time which will make me unable to come to your house and tell you just like I would like to about my case personally and how much I need your support. I have never been so sincere about asking for help as I am now. Since I am unable to do evanglist work or manual labor either, and while I have a wife and 4 children to support and not being able to work for them as I have in the past. To educate as I would like to I make this appeal from the depts of my heart. To every voter when you read this that you will say down in your heart that yu are voting with all your heart for the man that has been the peoples friend in the past, as it very well known in Whitley county that I was brought up a motherless boy from about 30 months old. My father was a poor farmer and lived about 9 miles from Williamsburg and I never had the care of a mother to guide me but made my way through the world as best I could. Beginning with the L & N at Corbin 1908 as a laborer at $1.26 per day, finally went on the road as brakeman in 1920. My health was so impaired I was forced to lay off. Then a few month later I took a job with the insurance company at $40 per week and built it up to about $7,0000 per year and became the Supt. in the Corbin territory. I was converted in 1924 felt the call to preach in 1926, so I worked of a day and evanglist work at night. Well in the 1st revival were 21 confessions 2nd revival were 45 confessions, 3rd revival were 62 confesssons, then the boss came to me and told me he didn't believe much in hereafter, that I would have to quit holding revivals or quit my job, so I soon made up my mind and quit my job as I was soon busy in winning lost souls ever since until I have brokedown maybe never to be able to work any more. I am not sorry that I gave up my job, or lost my health or sacrificed my living to win the lost, but I just want to be able to support my family and carry on to the hungry and needy on deserted mountains and valleys. I have borrowed money on my home to support my family while I preached for the poor until it looks as though I lose my home I have sold my last milk cow away from my children to pay debts. Friends if you ever did help a man who needed help don't fail to help me now. If I can redeem my home for my wife and little children, we can manage to get bread. So may I say before closing when you read this don't lay it down, take it to your friends, talk to them, if you know the worth of prayer.

Whitley's Next Representative

REV. L. B. MEADORS

The above is an excellent likeness of the Rev. L. B. Meadors, Representative-elect from the Whitley county district. Mr. Meadors is a native of the county, having been born and reared in the Cumberland Falls section where he has numerous relatives as well as in many other sections of the county.

Meadors Wins In Whitley.

Special to The Courier-Journal.

Williamsburg, Ky., Aug. 16.—On completion of the count in Whitley County L. B. Meadors won the Republican nomination for Representative with 3,431 votes to 2,076 for H. Speed Tye, incumbent. Malcolm Higgins finished third with 1,109, and D. C. Silcox trailed the field with 720.

Whitley County Courthouse

Photos of campain signs for County Judge.
Left: Linville Jr. and William on bike.
Right: Harriet standing and Linville seated.
Facing page: newspaper clips.

This Is A Reminder!

That You May Know Who My Relations Are

My father was Wm. B. Meadors who had two whole brothers Lewis Meadors married Millie Patrick, George Meadors married margaret Smith, two half brothers, Melt Durham, Horace Durham, two sisters Amy married John Wyatt, Martha Meabors married John Smith. My grandfather John Meadors who had five brothers, Joel Meadors married Nancy Patrick, Lewis married Susan Prewitt, Horace Meadors married Anda Patrick, Josiah Meadors married Liza Blakley, T. Meadors married Margaret Patrick, 4 sisters Betsey Meadors, married little Melt White, Polly Meadors married Lisha Inman, Sallie Meadors married Rev. Lewis Steely, Liza Meadors married Shelt Smith. My grandmother on my father's side was Relda White Meadors a daughter of Horac White and Amy Perkins, who had 3 brothers Jabe White married Betsey Taylor; Little Melt White married Betsey Meadors, Little Blue White married Rena Mayfield, two sisters Nancy White married Dan Wyatt Betsy White married Bill Haley. My mother was Lula Parker Meadors, who had 2 Brothers Rev. Lee B. Parker, Dr. J. H. Parker, 5 sisters Alice Parker, Manda Parker married Rube Hendricks, Dora Parker married Abe Cornett, Jaila Parker My grandfather on my mothers side was Geo. Parker, we had 2 brother Jess Parker married Rachel Patrick, Jim Parker who had 2 sisters Arlena Parker, Elizabeth Patrick My grandfather on my mothers side was Samie Parker, my grandmother on my mother's side was Liza Renfro, who had 3 brothers Jimmie Renfro, Jess Renfro, John Renfro, 1 sister Sara Renfro. My great grandmother on mother's side was Sara Jones, a daughter of Bennett Jones. My great great grand mothers was Pleas Meadors and Dicey McKee. My great great grand father and mother on my mothers side was Billy Davis and Sarah Roper.

Corbin, Ky. March 26, 1929

Rev L. B. Meadors,
Williamsburg, Kentucky

Above: Campaign card
Newspaper articles showing the vote tally and results.
Right: photo of the newly elected fiscal court. Linville is seated

MEADORS VICTORIOUS IN COUNTY JUDGE'S RACE

Smith, Shelton, Ellison and Faulkner Are Winners in Other Races For County Office

Although the campaign for county office got off to a slow start in Whitley County this year, it wound up last Saturday at the 52 voting places with all the warmth and vigor of former years.

Rev. L. B. Meadors, former Whitley County Representative in the State Legislature, defeated Joe Feather, his nearest opponent for County Judge, by a margin of 225 votes. This race developed in intensity during the final days of the campaign, but Mr. Feather was one of the very first to congratulate the winner Tuesday when the result became apparent.

In the race for Representative, Rev. J. F. Carr defeated Hugh C. Steely by a margin of 351 votes.

Walter Ray Smith was an easy winner in the race for County Attorney, polling a total of 4084 votes on the face of the unofficial returns, as compared with 2258 for Charles Stephens, who ran second. Albert Caddell, present incumbent, received a total of 1653 votes. R. C. Browning started in this race, but due to ill health was forced to withdraw two weeks ago.

There were nine applicants for the office of County Court Clerk, but the count disclosed that the race had simmered down and a neck and neck race between Tom Shelton and R. D. Evans. Mr. Shelton won by a margin of 125 votes, with Wolford Jones and John Stanfill running up pretty close to the leaders. A. J. Skeen also made a splendid showing in the clerk's race.

In the Sheriff's race its was Everett Ellison all the way through, although he was pitted against two unusually strong men. Mr. Ellison received a total of 4099 votes, while Mart West ran second with 2415 tallied to his credit. Ernest G. Hickey ran third with a total of 2117 votes.

John Faulkner, according to unofficial returns, received 2411 votes to win for Jailer, with T. J. Young running second with a total of 1508. Foreman Phillips was elected Coroner, defeating his nearest opponent Sandy Sears, 2249 to 1678.

E. S. Stringfield was unopposed for County Tax Commissioner, as was W. J. Moore for County Surveyor.

WHITLEY COUNTY'S NEW FISCAL COURT

—Whitley Republican Photo by H. A. Browning.

Pictured above are the men who will manage the County's fiscal affairs for the next four years. This photo was taken last Friday during their first session of the new year.

Front row, seated—Magistrate J. J. Johnson, Joe Feather, secretary; County Attorney Walter Ray Smith; County Judge L. B. Meadors; County Treasurer C. B. Upton and Magistrate D. W. Siler.

Back row, standing—Magistrates Raymond Meadors, Sid Peavely, W. F. Perkins, Lake Arnold, Garrett M. Castle and W. M. Bennett.

County Judge Elect L. B. Meadors Warns Slot Machine Operators

RESOLUTIONS

Do the good people of Whitley County appreciate the efforts of Judge Meadors in raiding the beer joints of our county? Will the good citizens of our county request their officers to cooperate with Judge in making our city a safe place for women to walk the streets after night? Shall the beer majority voters of our three signs continue to tantalize the counties? Shall the slot machines continue their gambling as law breakers? Shall the lewd women continue their advertisement on the streets and roads of our fair county? These are vital questions which the citizens of our county have a right to ask, and they have a right to ask that their wishes as expressed by their ballots be carried out by their officers and citizens. Why not let Judge Meadors know that your stand is with him?

Now in view of the public an-

Opinion Of Attorney General Read Before Capacity Attendance at Kiwanis Luncheon Today.

Judge-Elect L. B. Meadors of Whitley county declared war on gambling and slot machine operators today at noon in an address before a capacity attendance at the weekly Kiwanis club luncheon at the Wilbur hotel.

Introduced by I. O. Chitwood, Meadors declared "I will have jurisdiction over the slot machine as set out by law in this writ—the opinion of the Attorney General which I quote as follows:

"As to slot machines, if there is an element of chance, which there usually is, they are gambling devices.

"As to pin ball machines, if there is a prize offered involving an element of chance, where a person can get more for their money than they pay, or lose what they pay and get less, the Court of Ap-

A newspaper article announcing Linville's new effort to remove slot machines from Whitley County and a long article he wrote about his ideas.
The photos of slot machine, one of the models available in Whitley County at the time.

This is where the trouble began.

To the Citizens of Whitley County:

In keeping with the pledge I made to the good people of this county during my campaign for County Judge, I take this method of outlining my policy concerning the widespread operation of slot machines and other gambling devices in Whitley County. During the campaign I told the people I would do everything in my power to break up the wholesale operation of slot machines and I expect to keep that pledge.

The Kentucky Statutes expressly prohibit the setting up and operation of gambling machines and in order to refresh the minds of those who may be interested, I quote below several excerpts from the Statutes:

Section 1960 provides: "That whoever, with or without compensation, shall set up, carry on, keep, manage, operate or conduct, or shall aid or assist in setting up, carrying on, keeping, managing, operating or conducting a keno bank, faro bank or other machine or contrivance used in betting whereby money or other thing may be won or lost . . . . . shall be fined FIVE HUNDRED DOLLARS ($500.00) and costs and confined in the penitentiary not less than one nor more than three years; shall be deemed infamous after conviction, and be forever thereafter disqualified from exercising the right of suffrage, and from holding any office of honor, trust or profit, whether it be state, county city or municipal."

Right here I want to ask if anyone has ever heard of a slot machine being destroyed by any official in this county? It is common knowledge that the slot machine operators are only compelled to pay a nominal fine, three or four times a year, are permitted to keep and put their machines in operation again after each term of court, and thus their nefarious business continues to flourish in the face of Section 1962 of the Kentucky Statutes which says they shall be destroyed.

Section 1962 provides: "Any bank, table, contrivance or machine, or articles used for carrying on such game or games, or any of them, mentioned or included in Section 1960 of this chapter, together with all money or other thing staked or exhibited to allure persons to bet, may be seized by any MAGISTRATE, SHERIFF, CONSTABLE OR POLICE OFFICER of a city or town, with or without a warrant, and upon conviction of the person setting up or keeping the game, machine, bank or contrivance, such money or other things shall be forfeited for the use of the Commonwealth, and such table, machine or articles shall be burned or destroyed. And though NO PERSON shall be convicted as the setterup; or keeper of such table or game, machine, bank or contrivance, yet if a jury shall, in summary proceedings, find that the money, table, bank, machine or contrivance, or other things, were used or intended to be used for the purpose of such gaming, they shall be so condemned and forfeited."

It would seem, from the above two Sections of the Kentucky Statutes, that our officers have a duty to perform, and I, for one, expect to perform my duty. I am serving notice on all slot machine operators here and now that they can not operate in Whitley County after I take office on January 1. Those who want to avoid prosecution under the Statutes above quoted should arrange to take their machines out of this county before I go into office. I think it only fair to warn them, and this is my way of so doing. Those who try to operate slot machines after the first of the year may expect to have the machines destroyed as the law provides. There will be no compromise, in so far as I am concerned. The gambling machines must go.

It is my ardent hope that I may be able to render my county a real service during the next four years, and I appeal to all the good citizens and church people to stand by me in my efforts to enforce the law. Our county is only what we make it. Let's keep it clean.

Your friend,

L. B. MEADORS.

Not thinking someone might object.

Left: photo of two country boys who might have been offended by the removal of slot machines.
Right: An article about Linville announcing that he would give up his post as County Judge in order to concentrate on his preaching.
A photo of Linville in a cemetary looking sad.

Judge Meadors Resigns Post Saturday P. M.

1940

Announces That He Will Go Back Into His Ministry.

1940

WILLIAMSBURG, Ky., May 11. (Special)—Giving as his reason "my sacred obligation to the call of the ministry", County Judge L. B. Meadors resigned from office Saturday afternoon.

The action was taken at 2:30 P. M. yesterday. Judge Meadors made known his resignation in a speech over a loud speaker at the Whitley county courthouse. In the resignation address, Judge Meadors said he had found that his preaching and the duties of a judge did not mix, that he was unable to continue his official duties and at the same time find energy and time for the ministry.

He cited personal history, going back to July 16, 1927, when he resigned a job which was paying him about seven thousand dollars a year, because he had heard the call to preach. He had interrupted his career as a minister to become interested in politics, but had found that he did not now have time to devote to his religious duties.

He announced that he would now be actively engaged in preaching.

Judge Meadors filed the record of his resignation with County Court Clerk Tom Shelton, and turned over the keys of the office to him. He mailed a copy to Frankfort.

Governor Keen Johnson will name a successor. The appointed judge will hold office till after the general election in November, and thereafter until the end of 1941 unless somebody makes the race for the unexpired term.

Judge Meadors' statement:

"Joshua 24:15 'Whereas God has made known his will in my life that I shall preach his everlasting gospel to a lost and benighted world.'

"Realing the position I now hold as County Judge of Whitley County is of a confining nature thus depriving me of carrying out his will for which I shall answer at the day of judgement and reaching the place where I must decide for the future;

"Whereas after due consideration and feeling my sacred obligation to the call of the ministry, I now tender my resignation to the clerk of Whitley County effective today on this 11th day of May, 1940.

Signed: L. B. MEADORS."

L.B. moved his family to Knoxvillle on September 16, 1945. They rented a house at 35 Emerral Street, living upstairs. He opened aa grocery business downstairs run by his two oldest sons, L.B. Jr and my father, Billy Harold. The photo below is the house still standing today. Also a clip from the Street Directory showing this.

Listing from Knoxville City Directory, 1945

Meadors Bros Grocery (W H and L B Meadors) 135 E Emerald av
" J Irene Miss student r 135 E Emerald av (2d fl)
" Linville B Rev (Harriett H) r 135 E Emerald av (2d fl)
" Linville B Jr (Meadors Bros Grocery) r 135 E Emerald av (2d fl)
Wm H (Meadors Bros Grocery) r

Linville and Harriet relaxing at their home on Magnolia Street in Knoxville, date unknown.

On April 13, 1958, L.B. moved his family to Jacksonville, Florida where many of his children and grandchildren lived. They stayed there until they fell ill, and both returned to their beloved Tennessee for their terminal care.

They are buried side by side in Alcoa, Tennessee.

Rev. Linville Barton Meadors Sr.
1895–1980 • GDFK-YBT
Marriage: 2 January 1922
Winchester, Clark, Kentucky, United States
Harriet Hatcher
1903–1995 • LTB1-QC2

William Bluford Meadors
1863–1934 • LYHP-K9W
Marriage: 10 September 1881
Whitley, Kentucky, United States
Lucinda C Parker
1865–1898 • 2W31-J8B

John W Meadors
1827–1863 • LYHG-QN3
Marriage: 27 July 1852
Whitley, Kentucky, United States
Mary Surrelda White
1828–1892 • KHC2-DMW

William Bluford Meadors
Lucinda C. Parker

Whitley county was formed January 17, 1818, from a section of Knox County and was named in honor of Col. William Whitley, a Kentucky pioneer and Indian fighter. The county seat, Williamsburg, was originally called Whitley Courthouse.

In April 1759, explorer Dr. Thomas Walker and his party entered the Whitley County area at Blake's Fork Creek. Raiding parties of Indians frequently attacked and killed hunters and trappers. Among those killed, probably by Cherokee, were Joseph Johnson at Lynn Camp and the son of Joe Tye on Big Poplar Creek. In 1786 Indians attacked the large group of settlers known as McNitt's company and killed twenty-one of them in the area between the Big and Little Laurel Rivers.

In the 1860s, Whitley County, Kentucky, was deeply affected by the Civil War, with skirmishes in and around Williamsburg, including Confederate Scott's Raid in July 1863.

Photo right: Cumberland Falls in Whitley County
Left: Union soldiers following Scott's raid.
Facing: a photograph of Williamsburg, county seat of Whitley County, circa 1880

William Bluford Meadors was born 16 Nov 1865 in Kentucky, and died at age 69, on January 7, 1934, in Whitley County, Kentucky of apoplexy. He is buried in Steely Cemetery in Redbird, Whitley County.

He was married three times, the first, to Lucinda Parker, which makes him my great grandfather. Lucinda grew up in the Lower Regions, in Whitley County. They were married September 14, 1881, at George Parker's house, Whitley, Kentucky. She was 16.

Lucinda's name is variously recorded as Lulu, Louisa, and others. She was born May 17, 1865 in Whitley County, and died January 25, 1898 and is buried in Redbird Cemetery in Whitley.

In the 1860 census, Bluford was listed as 6 years old living with his parents in Lower, Whitley. In 1870, at age 16, the family lived in Marsh Creek, Kentucky. In 1910, he owned his own farm "free and clear." His youngest child, Linvil Meadors, my grandfather, was 5. In 1910, he lived on Meadows Road, Jellico Creek, Whitley, Kentucky.

Top: photo of Bluford Meadows,
Below: his signature.
Left: excerpts from the U.S.Census Reports from 1910, 1920, and 1930.
Facing: a photograph of Bluford as a grandfather, others unknown as is the date.

1910 Census

1920 Census

1930 Census

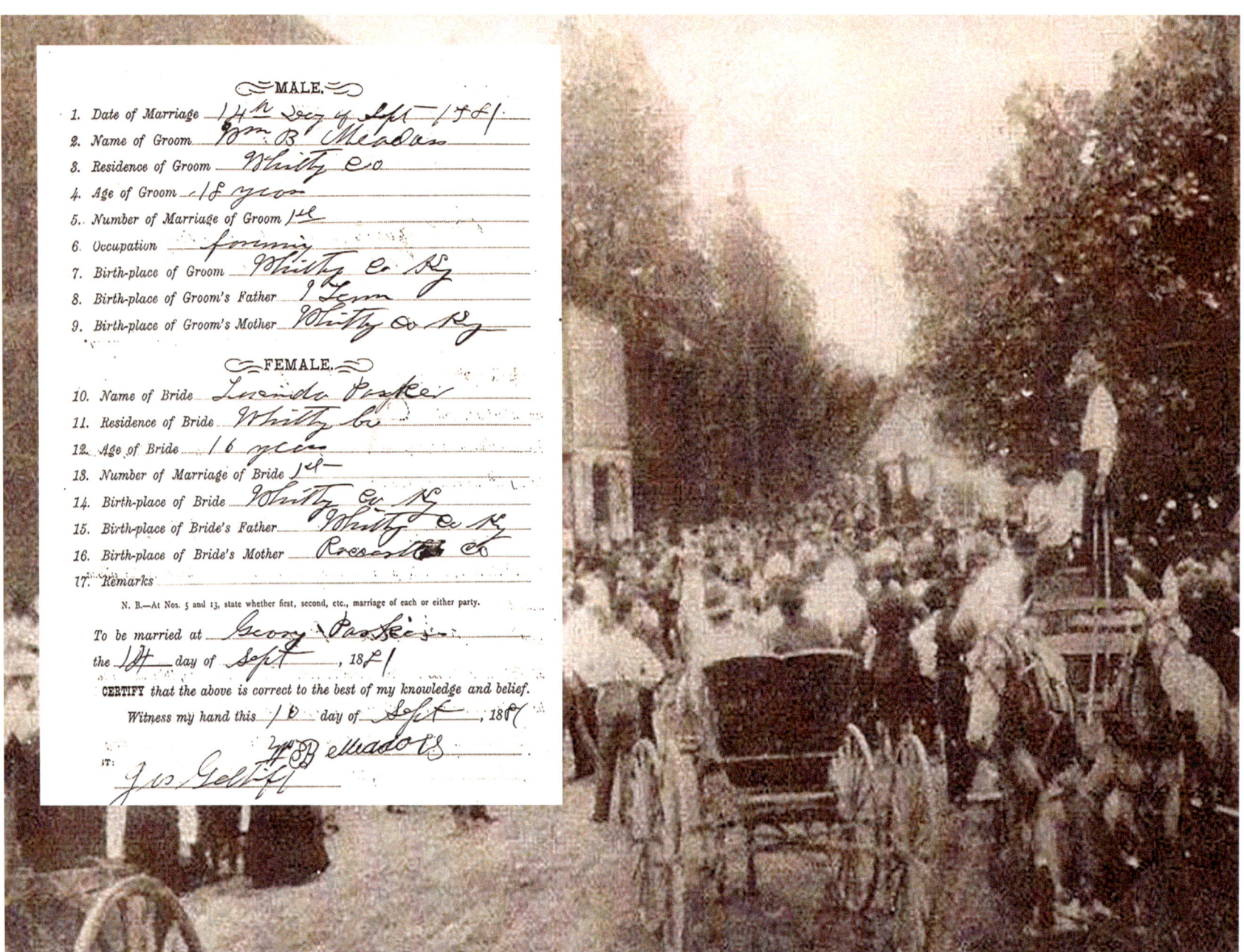

MALE.
1. Date of Marriage 14th day of Sept 1881
2. Name of Groom Wm B Meadors
3. Residence of Groom Whitly Co
4. Age of Groom 18 year
5. Number of Marriage of Groom 1st
6. Occupation farming
7. Birth-place of Groom Whitly Co Ky
8. Birth-place of Groom's Father 9 Tenn
9. Birth-place of Groom's Mother Whitly Co Ky

FEMALE.
10. Name of Bride Lucinda Parker
11. Residence of Bride Whitly Co
12. Age of Bride 16 year
13. Number of Marriage of Bride 1st
14. Birth-place of Bride Whitly Co Ky
15. Birth-place of Bride's Father Whitly Co Ky
16. Birth-place of Bride's Mother Roccastle Co
17. Remarks

N.B.—At Nos. 5 and 13, state whether first, second, etc., marriage of each or either party.

To be married at George Parker's
the 14 day of Sept, 1881

CERTIFY that the above is correct to the best of my knowledge and belief.

Witness my hand this 10 day of Sept, 1881

Wm B Meadors
Jos Geltry

My Great Grandfather, Bluford Meadows.
My father is the baby sitting on his grandfather's knee,
in a house somewhere in Whitley County, probably Craig Road.
Linville Jr., is in the middle and Irene stands to the right.
Facing page is a photo from Whitley County early 1900's.
Also Bluford and Lucinda's marriage license.

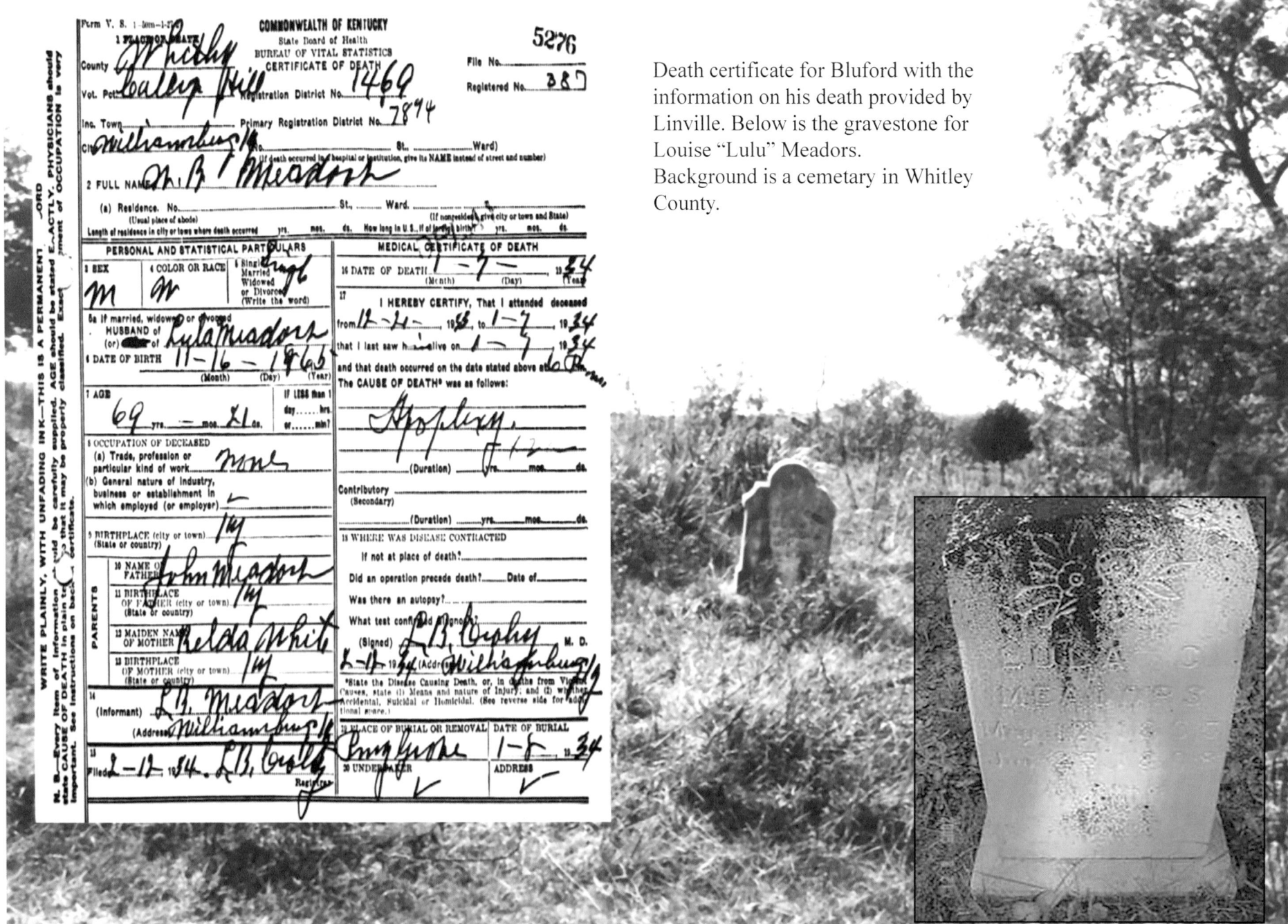

Death certificate for Bluford with the information on his death provided by Linville. Below is the gravestone for Louise "Lulu" Meadors.
Background is a cemetary in Whitley County.

Last Will and Testament of William Bluford Meadors

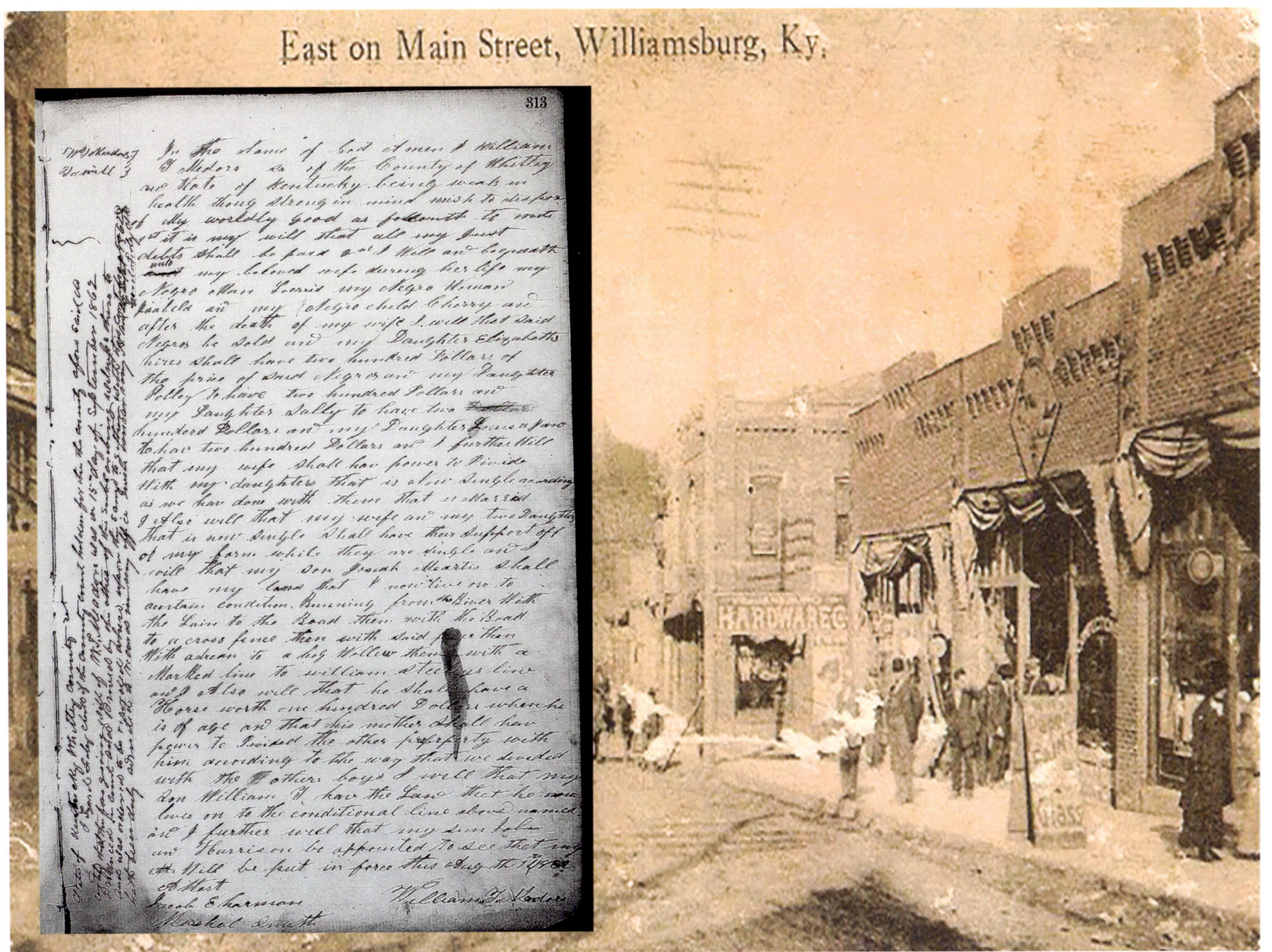

William Bluford Meadors	John W Meadors	William Troy Meadors Sr.
1863-1934 • LYHP-K9W	1827-1863 • LYHG-QN3	1803-1862 • LHQZ-7D9
Marriage: 10 September 1881 Whitley, Kentucky, United States	Marriage: 27 July 1852 Whitley, Kentucky, United States	Marriage: 19 October 1823 Williamsburg, Whitley, Kentucky, United St...
Lucinda C Parker	**Mary Surrelda White**	**Sarah Smith**
1865-1898 • 2W31-J8B	1828-1892 • KHC2-DMW	1807-1893 • L6QP-4CJ

Pvt 3rd Class

John W. Meadors,

and

Mary Surrelda "Polly" White

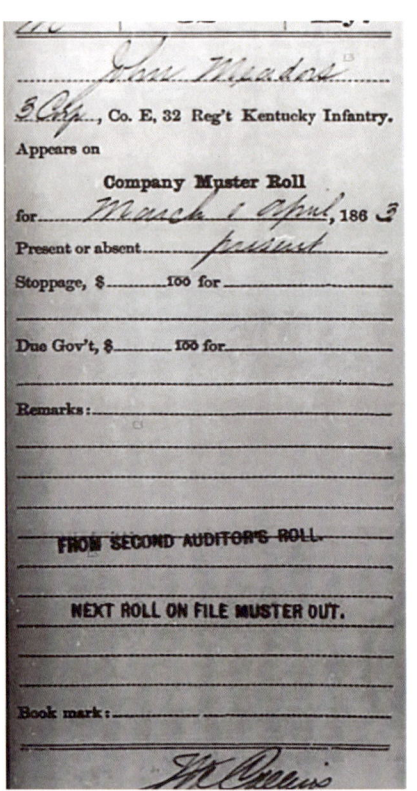

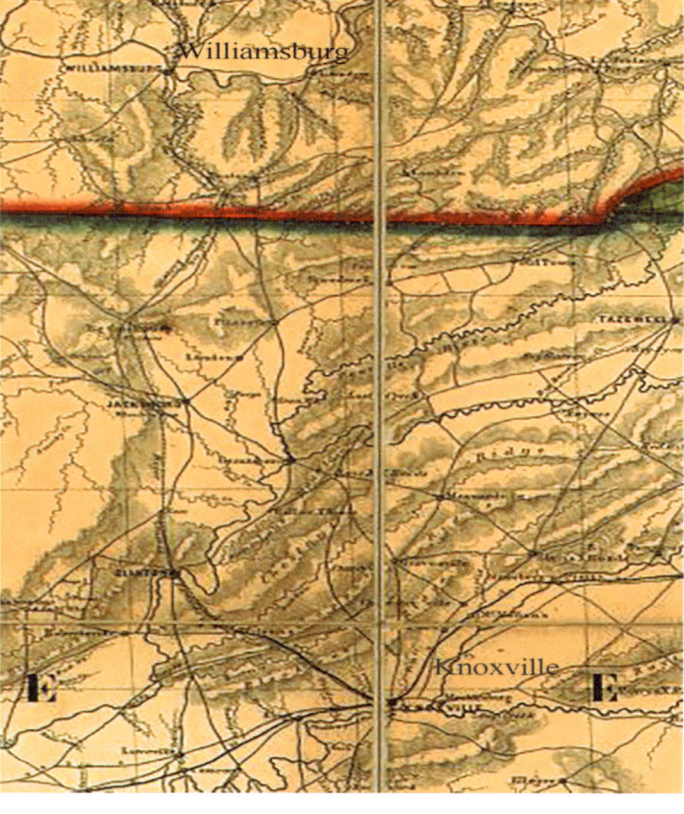

Meace, Jacob		Pvt	F	32nd Ky. Infantry
Meadors, John		Corpl	E	32nd Ky. Infantry
Meadors, Joseph		Pvt	E	32nd Ky. Infantry

John W. Meadors was born on April 22, 1827, in Wayne, Kentucky. He married Mary Surrelda "Polly" White on July 27, 1852, in Whitley, Kentucky. They had seven children over twenty-one years. He died on June 22, 1863, in Whitley, Kentucky, at the age of 36, and was buried at Redbird Cemetery in Whitley. She died there on March 29, 1892 and was buried in Steely Cemetery, Redbird, Whitley, Kentucky.

On December 12th 1862, he enlisted in the Union Army at Camp Burnside, Kentucky, as part of the 32nd Infantry. His final rank was private 3rd class.

Camp Burnside in Kentucky was established by Union General Ambrose Burnside as a military camp and supply depot. The camp was located on the Cumberland River, near present-day Burnside, Kentucky. Camp Burnside served as a crucial supply depot for the Union Army in the region.

John and Mary Surrelda "Polly" White Meadors

The 32nd Kentucky Infantry Regiment was organized at Frankfort and Camp Burnside, Kentucky in August 1862. The regiment was primarily involved in guard and scouting duties in Western Kentucky, including Hopkinsville, Camp Burnside, Danville, Lexington, Somerset, Stanford, and Lebanon. It was mustered out of service beginning on May 28, 1863, and ending on August 12, 1863.

The Civil War Soldiers and Sailors database lists 1,167 men on its roster for this unit, of which 43 died. All died of disease. In Kentucky and across the Civil War armies, a soldier dying of disease was most likely to succumb to diarrhea/dysentery, followed by typhoid fever, malaria, and pneumonia.

An estimated 74–125,000 Kentuckians served as Union soldiers, and an estimated 25–40,000 served as Confederate soldiers.

Left, John's Muster Roll Card; a map of Kentucky and Tennessee, bottom left, an excerpt from the military roll of Union soldiers The soldier is unknown. Right: thought to be a photo of John and Polly, date unknown. Below: Polly's gravestone.

Slavery in Kentucky

Drawing of the Lynching of a Black man in somewhere in Kentucky

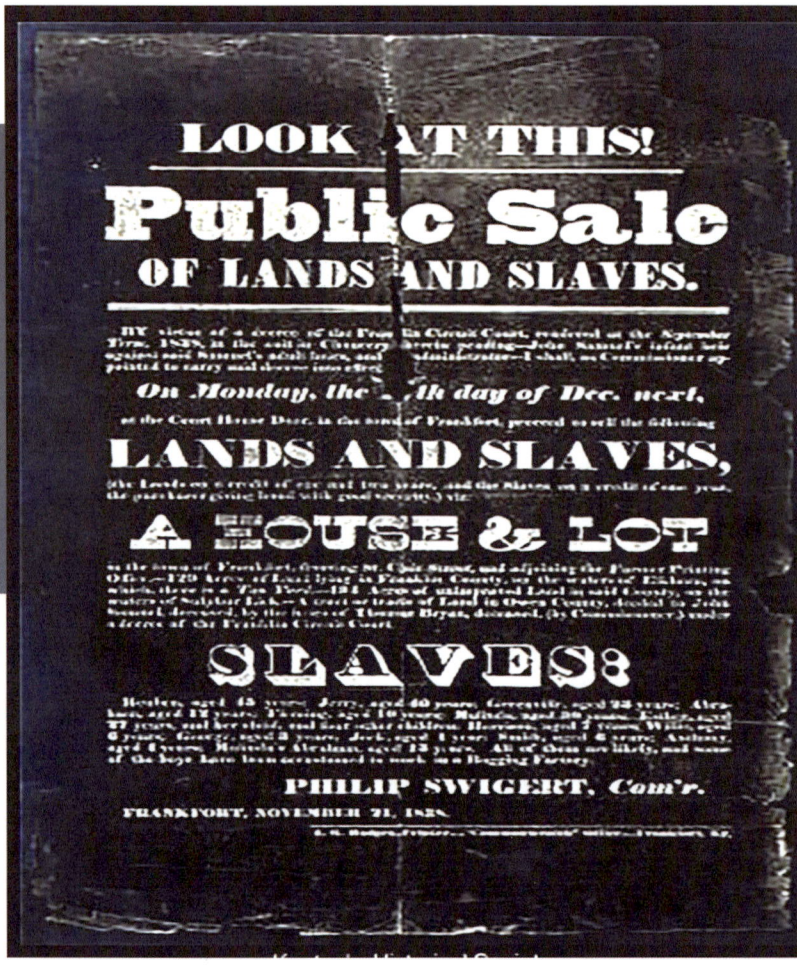

Poster for a Slave Sale in Frankfort, Kentucky

Photo of field slaves

TO THE PEOPLE, Who wish to do Right!

A flyer decrying slavery and offering an alternative.
A typical Union soldier.

State of Kentucky

1850 Slave Schedule
141 slave owners
447 Black slaves
131 Mulatto slaves
3 free Blacks

1860 Slave Schedule
212 slave owners
720 Black slaves
259 Mulatto slaves
22 free Blacks

1870 U.S. Federal Census
528 Blacks
177 Mulattoes

On May 16, 1861, Kentucky enacted a resolution declaring neutrality in the Civil War, with no allegiance to either the United States or the Confederacy.
In September, Kentucky declared full allegiance to the United States.

William Troy Meadors
Sarah Sally "Sarry" Smith

John W Meadors	**William Troy Meadors Sr.**	Thomas Meadors Jr.
1827-1863 • LYHG-QN3	1803-1862 • LHQZ-7D9	1771-1818 • LZKD-XNJ
Marriage: 27 July 1852	Marriage: 19 October 1823	Marriage: about 1794
Whitley, Kentucky, United States	Williamsburg, Whitley, Kentucky, United St	Virginia, United States
Mary Surrelda White	**Sarah Smith**	Elizabeth Martin
1828-1892 • KHC2-DMW	1807-1893 • L6QP-4CJ	1779-1861 • L4BT-45R

William Troy Meadors Sr was born on May 11,1803 in Anson, North Carolina and died of natural causes on September 9th, 1862, aged 59 in Redbird, Whitley. He married Sarah Sally Smith in Williamsburg, Whitley County on October 19th, 1823. They had 11 children. In 1804, as a baby, his family moved across the Cumberland Gap, from his home in Anson County, NC to Knox County, Kentucky.

1860 Census
He owned real estate worth $1,100 and personal estate worth $3,000. He was 57.

1862 Will
In the Name of God Amen I William T. Medors Sr of the County of Whitley and State of Kentucky being weak in health though strong in mind wish to dispose of My worldly Goods as followeth to wit 1st it is my will that all my just debts shall be paid 2nd I will and bequeath unto my beloved wife during her life

My Negro Man Loerris , my Negro Woman Isabela and my Negro child Cherry

and after the death of my wife I will that said Negros be sold and my Daughter Elizabeth's hires [sic] shall have two hundred Dollars of the price of said Negros and my Daughter Polly to have two hundred Dollars and my Daughter Sally

This is the only documented account of our Meadows family as enslavers I have been able to find.

Sarry Smith

to have two hundred Dollars and my Daughter Louisa Jane to have two hundred Dollars and I further Will that my wife shall have power to Divide with my daughters that is Now Single acording as we hav done with them that is Married I Also will that my wife and my two Daughters that is now Single Shall have their support off of my farm while they are single and I will that my son Josiah Meartis shall have my land that I now live on to a certain condition. Running from the River with the Lain to the Road then with the Road to a cross fence then with said fence then With a drean to a hog Wollow then with a Marked line to William Steeleys line and I Also will that he shall have a Horse worth one hundred Dollars when he is of age and that his mother Shall have power to Divide the other property with him according to the way that we divided with the other boys I will that my son William T. have the Land that he now lives on to the conditional line above named, and I further will that my son John and Harrison be appointed to see that my Will be put in force this Aug the 11th 1862
Signed William T. Medors

Sarah Sally "Sarry" Smith was born August 25, 1807 in Knox County, Kentucky. She died there on September 3rd, 1893 of a broken hip, "and the infirmities of age." Her ancestors arc said to have been from Yorktown, Virginia. They made their way to Lincoln County about 1785. Our Sarry Smith would spend most of her life in Whitley County, Kentucky. Her grave is in Redbird Cemetery next to the Cumberland River runs. Sarah Smith Meadors was a member of Redbird Baptist Church. She had been married to William Troy Meadors for 38 years when she became a widow at the age of 55. She would live for 31 years as a widow.

Gravestones of Sarry, left, and William Troy, on the right.

Thomas Jefferson Meadors, Jr.
Elizabeth "Betsy" Martin

William Troy Meadors Sr.
1803-1862 • LHQZ-7D9
Marriage: 19 October 1823
Williamsburg, Whitley, Kentucky, United St...
Sarah Smith
1807-1893 • L6QP-4CJ

Thomas Meadors Jr.
1771-1818 • LZKD-XNJ
Marriage: about 1794
Virginia, United States
Elizabeth Martin
1779-1861 • L4BT-45R

Thomas Meador Sr
1736-1826 • LZJY-HC1
Marriage: about 1760
South Carolina, United States
Keziah Moberly
1747-1830 • MW8N-YK9

Thomas Jefferson Meadors, Jr., was born in 1771 in Anson, North Carolina, British Colonial America. On October the 16th, 1794, he married Elizabeth Martin Todd and they had eleven children. He died November 28, 1818 and is buried Jellico Creek Cemetery, Williamsburg Whitley County.

Elizabeth "Betsy" Martin Todd was born September 27, 1779, in North Carolina. She died April 16, 1861 in Whitley County. She is buried in Old Jellico Creek Cemetery, Whitley County.

Betsy's gravestone

Their first five children were born in North Carolina before 1804, when the family moved to Knox County, Kentucky. It seems that when they walked through the Cumberland Gap that they were with a large family group, which included his parents, Keziah Moberly Meadors & Thomas Meadors Sr. as well.

Minutes of Cumberland River Baptist Church, Knox, KY, 4 Sat Nov 4th,1808, Whitley, KY.
"The church met according to adjuournment and after worship proceeded to business as follows: A Door was opened and received by experience Archibald Blake, Thomas Meadows, Elisha Inman, Elias Kidd, Dicy Saunders, Mary Morgan, Morning Inman and Sally Inman and so adjourned until meeting in course."

War of 1812

Thomas Jefferson Meadors served in the military in 1812 when he was 41 years old. He was enlisted in Hall's Regiment of the Tennessee Volunteers. He was discharged with the rank of Sergeant.

The 1st regiment was part of Andrew Jackson's expedition to Natchez; this regiment had a complement of about 620 men (the average company having between fifty and seventy soldiers). Each company was assigned a fife and drummer. There were two rifle companies (Captains Bledsoe and Kennedy) which had buglers instead of the fife and drummer. After the abortive mission at Natchez, this unit was dismissed at Columbia, Tennessee in April 1814.

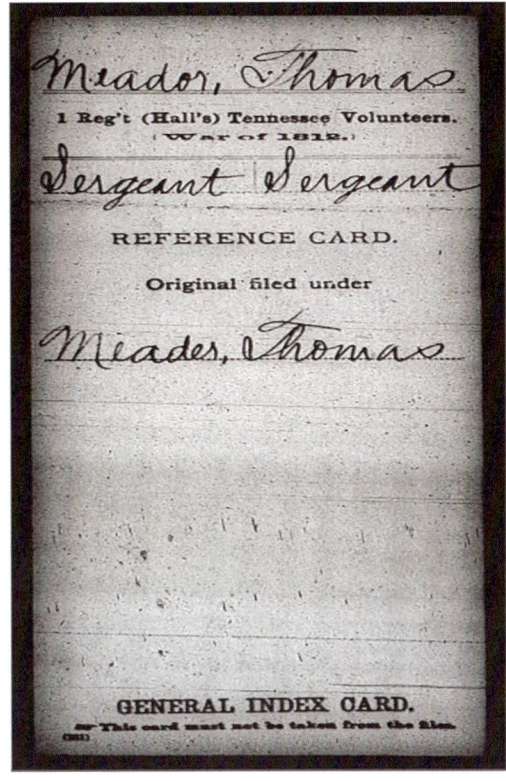

Index card for Thomas Meadors in Hall's Tennessee Volunteers. Below, two renditions of battles of the War of 1812.

Thomas Meador Sr., and Keziah Moberly

Thomas Meadors Jr.
1771–1818 • LZKD-XNJ
Marriage: about 1794
Virginia, United States
Elizabeth Martin
1779–1861 • L4BT-45R

Thomas Meador Sr
1736–1826 • LZJY-HC1
Marriage: about 1760
South Carolina, United States
Keziah Moberly
1747–1830 • MW8N-YK9

Jason Meador
1704–1776 • L5LF-RGL
Marriage: 1729
Caroline, Virginia, British Colonial America
Elizabeth Stone
1709–1778 • LVRX-GY5

Thomas' parents, Jason Meadors and Anne Stone Meadors, took their six children to Anson County, North Carolina around November 1772. Somewhere along the way, they met the Moberly family and became close. Five of Jason Meadors' children married into the Moberly family.

Thomas Meadors married Keziah Moberly when she was just a teenager. Records show they were living in Craven Co., SC on November 2, 1772 and owned land near the Hills and Moberlys. During their very long marriage, they would have twelve children.

Left: a photograph of present day Cumberland Gap.
Facing: a drawing of a mule-drawn covered wagon making its way across the Cumberland Gap.

Thomas Sr and Keziah and their large family migrated to Kentucky in 1804, hiking on foot, a trip of 400 miles. They would have crossed the Great Smoky Mountains and Cumberland Gap. The Meadors settled in the Marsh Creek area of Knox County, Kentucky. On the 1810 Federal Census for Knox Co., we see the couple living with their teenage son, while nearby, the Thomas Meadors Jr. family has their own home with many children. Other family members are living in the neighborhood.

Thomas Meadors Jr. died in 1818. His bereaved parents had to watch their son be buried while his children were still young. Thomas Meadors Sr. lived for another eight years, until 1826.

Keziah Moberly

Born 1747, Lunenburg County, Virginia Colony of British America
Died 1830 • Whitley, Kentucky Buried Jellico Creek, Whitley, Kentucky, United States

The name Keziah means 'cinnamon bark', referring to the Hebrew word 'to scrape off'
Job gave thename to one of his daughters born after his restoration
following the trials he faced in the first part of his life.
The name has been taken to **symbolize female equality,**
since all of Job's three daughters received an inheritance from their father,
an unusual circumstance in a time period when women and men were not treated equally

Above: photos of typical family farms in Knox County Kentucy in the early 1800s.
Facing: a composite photograph of the Cumberland Gap.

Cumberland Gap

More About Thomas Meador Sr.

To the Honuorable the General Assembly of North Carolina

The Petition of the Inhabitants of Anson County Humbly Seteth forth that they are Informed that at the last General assembly there was a Separate Election and General Muster Established in the County aforesaid, contrary to their Knowledge or wish &C - - - And that your Petition further shewith, that Said County is Compact perhaps as any in the State aforesaid, and the Courthouse Situated within a few miles of its Centre, And that the County has been at Great Expense Erecting Bridges &C- that no Inconveniency hath yet arisen nor can arise on that head, and we Humbly Conceive that Said Separate Election and General Muster was Erected from Sinister Views, and not from motives of publick good and that the Seperation is only attended with unnecessary Expenses,- - Now so it is we Pray your Honours in your Wisdoms to take the case under your wise Consideration and repeal Said act, or as much therof as to Granting a Separate Election and General Muster in the County aforesaid and that they Elections and General Musters in the County aforesaid, be Consolidated and held at the same place and in the same manner they were before such Law passed, as Such other Relief in the Premises as to your Honours in your Wisdom may Seem Just and Right, and your petitioners as In duty Bound .
Signed by Thomas Meador Sr and others.

Nov the 8th 1800...Thomas Meader...

On The Sale of Land as described,

Between Thomas Meadows Sr. of Knox County, Kentucky and Pleasant Meadows of same place Thomas Meadows bargains and sells land unto Pleasant Meadows Land on Cumberland River Beginning on John Pruitt's corner a dogwood and sourwood. Thence up the river with it's meanders East 14 poles. Thence South 55 East 26 poles. Thence South 20 east 36 poles. Thence S 8 East 22 poles. Thence S 10 W 31 poles ..Thence S 16 W 18 poles .Thence S 24 W 32 poles.. Thence South 22 W 60 poles. Thence South 17 W 49 poles to a black oak and maple. Thence South 49 E poles to a black oak and John Pruitt's line. Thence North 32 poles East 60 poles with said line to a black oak. Thence North 48 E 30 poles to a pine. Thence North 24 E 116 poles to the Beginning Containing 100 acres more or less but it is to be understood that the said Thomas Meadows is to have possession during his and his wife's natural life time."

Signed Thomas Meadows Witness James F. Ballenger DC Recorded 28 Aug 1819.

The Regulator Rebellion

The Regulator Movement: In the late 1760s, farmers in the North Carolina backcountry grew increasingly frustrated with corrupt officials who were levying excessive taxes and fees. They protested these injustices, calling themselves "Regulators" who sought to regulate public officials. The Regulators protested and fomented insurrection for several years. The protests escalated into armed confrontation as the colonial government refused to negotiate and prepared to suppress the movement.

The Battle of Alamance. On May 16, 1771, about 2,000 untrained Regulators fought the colonial militia, led by Governor William Tryon. Tryon had recruited about 1,000 militia to take on the Regulators. On the day of the Battle, nearly 2,000 Regulators fought against the militia; however, despite having nearly double the number of men, the Regulators were quickly defeated. They had insufficient supplies, limited weapons, and were lacking a strong system of leadership which, coupled with the military training and preparedness of the militia, resulted in a swift defeat.

Despite the military defeat, the battle was seen by many as a struggle for political and economic fairness. Its publicization in newspapers throughout the colonies drew attention to the cause, and the Regulators were hailed by some as martyrs to the American cause

Above: drawing of the Regulators agitating.
Below: drawing of the Battle of Alamance.

Jason Meadors, Sr.

Elizabeth Harrison Stone

	Jason Meador	
Thomas Meador Sr	1704–1776 • L5LF-RGL	**John Meador**
1736–1826 • LZJY-HC1		1658–1721 • L89D-GTT
Marriage: about 1760	Marriage: 1729	
South Carolina, United States	Caroline, Virginia, British Colonial America	
Keziah Moberly	**Elizabeth Stone**	**Mary Francis Awbrey**
1747–1830 • MW8N-YK9	1709–1778 • LVRX-GY5	1665–1721 • PST7-XDV

Jason Meadors, Sr., was born in Essex, Virginia, British Colonial America in 1704. He may have been a twin to Job Meadors. He married Elizabeth Stone on June 10th, 1729 in Caroline County, Virginia, British Colonial America.

He died June 10th, 1776, and was buried in Jason Meadow Cemetery, Anson, North Carolina. The Jason Meadow homeplace is on Gordon's Mountain, located in southern Anson Co., NC. Jason MEADORS, Sr. and Jason MEADORS, Jr. were Regulators in 1768-1769 in North Carolina or Virginia.

Jason is recorded as a Quaker, on May 9th, 1743 at the Cedar Creek Monthly Meeting in Caroline County. He attended services at Richmond and Cedar Creek Monthly Meetings.

In 1743, (1743 Nov 11 - Caroline Co, VA Court Order Book 1740-1746 - p. 237) Jonas and brother Jason were indicted by the Caroline County Grand Jury for not attending St. Margaret's, the local Anglican parish church, and fined 5 shillings or 50 pounds of tobacco each. The men stated they were Quakers, and the charges were dismissed.

Being a Quaker, Jason refused to bear arms and was fined. Some of his property was seized to pay the fine, and he was the denied the use of his horse for one year.

Jason Meador followed his brother Jonas to Caroline County, VA, and purchased land there in 1739.

On 12 January 1747 Jason Meador was granted a patent of 551 acres in Amelia County at the head of Sandy Creek.

In 1751 Jason Meador sold his land in Amelia County, VA and purchased 200 acres on the Little Otter River near the Blue Ridge Mountains, then Jason bought another 300 acres there in 1757.

About 1759-60 the two families formed a wagon train with the Moberly family and trekked to Craven County, South Carolina.

Left: Last Will and Testament of John Meadors Sr.
Below: Quaker Meeting circa 1700s.

Left: photo of present day Gordon's Mountain in Anson County, site of Jason and Elizabeth's home.
Below: map showing the location

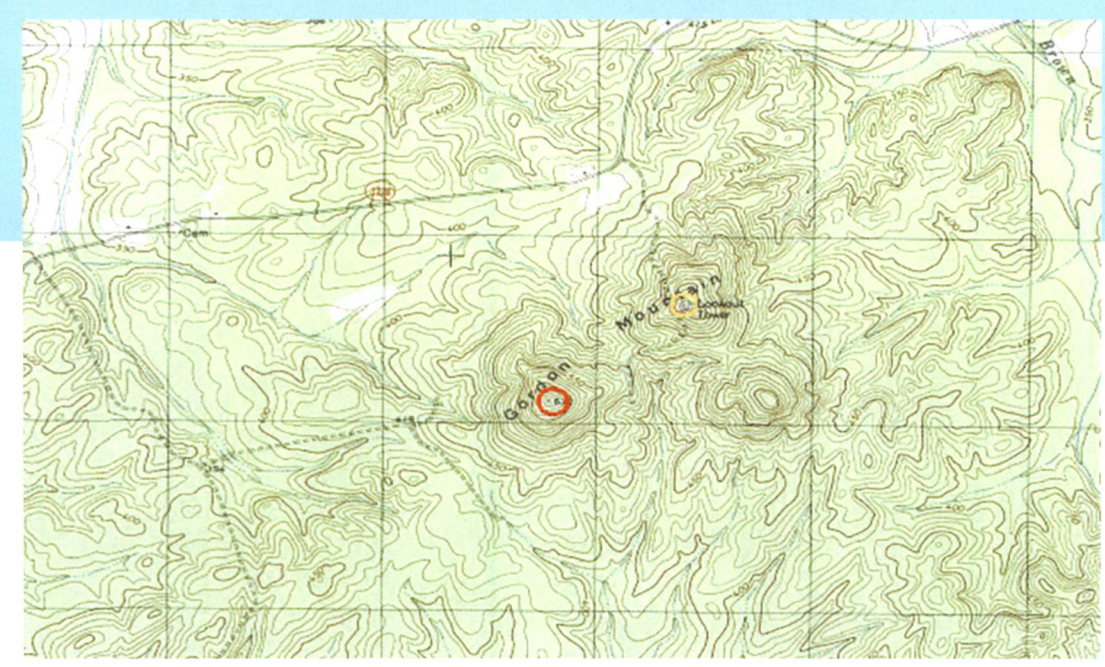

Last Will and Testament of Jason Meador

In the name of God Amen. I Jason Meador of the County of Anson in the province of North Carolina being in perfect since and memory Thanks be to the Almighty God for the same but Calling to mind the Certainty of Death and uncertainty of life knowing that it is appointed that I should Die I give my Soul to the almighty God and my body to the Earth from whence it came and ordain This my Last Will and Testament as following to say it is my Desire that all my Debts to be paid by the Disrefsions of my Executors as following. I give and bequeath in promisis I Give unto my beloved wife Elizabeth the plantation as I now possess and all other my substance During her natural Life and at her Decease it is my will that the sd. plantation and Tract of land Ducend unto my children it is also my will and desire that my said wife Elizabeth keep in possession and enjoy all the rest of my Estate real and personal During her natural Life and at her Decease to be Divided as hereafter Directed. I give unto my eldest son Lewis five shillings sterling and also Drucilla, Marion and Thomas one Shilling sterling Each. Then it is my Will, that at the Decease of my wife Elizabeth that my Plantation and Land and other substance be Equally Divided amongst several Children herein named Lewis Jason Job and Mariah to them and their heirs and assigns forever. Lastly I do constitute and appoint my Beloved wife Elizabeth my son Lewis and Job sole Executors of this my Last Will and Testament hereby Revoking Disinniling and making void all former and other wills, by me heretofore made ratifying and holding The above primisis as Witness my hand and seal this Twenty Third Day of March Anno Domini one Thousand Seven hundred and Seventy four.

John Meadors
Elizabeth Ann White

John Meadors was born July 31, 1658 in Charles Parrish, York County, Virginia, British Colonial America. In February 1678, he married Elizabeth Ann White at Old Rappahannock, Virginia, British Colonial America. He died November 12, 1721 in Essex County, Virginia.

Jason Meador
1704-1776 • L5LF-RGL
Marriage: 1729
Caroline, Virginia, British Colonial America

Elizabeth Stone
1709-1778 • LVRX-GY5

John Meador
1658-1721 • L89D-GTT

Mary Francis Awbrey
1665-1721 • PST7-XDV

Thomas Meador Jr
1634-1662 • LJ58-5PJ

Sarah Hoskins
1637-1674 • M45Q-44R

John spent his childhood with his siblings, mother and step father, Henry Awbrey, on Awbrey's plantation on the upper reaches of Hoskins Creek. Nearby, hostile Indians had raided a neighboring plantation and brutally murdered a young man there. During his childhood years, the Indians were forced deep into the forest.

In the 1650's, the Quaker religion was being introduced in Virginia. The "Quiet Contemplation" of the Quakers and their reliance upon personal enlightenment found common ground with the self-reliant planters on the frontier. Despite the disapproval of the Anglican church, Quakerism spread rapidly throughout the settlements. Whether or not John himself became a Quaker is not known. However, two of his children, Jonas and Jason, did become Quakers.

20 April 1687, p. 558. "John Meador, 640 acres (Old) Rappahannock County: South side Rappahannock River on Beverday Southwest at the head of Hoskins' C reek, Beginning on South side of the old Beverday Southwest, near an Indian path; to a small island & etc.; assigned to Thomas Medors, 7 Aug 1659; & granted him 9 April 1664; 190 acres for transporting of 4 persons: John Chambers, Joseph Callaway, Robert Duell, John Warrener." (Land grants were given for each person a citizen paid for their voyage to the Colonies.)

By the early 1690's John Meador held at least 1095 acres of land centered on a grant of 450 acres and straddling Hoskins Creek just upstream from the location now called Cheatwood Millpond.

Inventory OF John Meador, Sr. Essex County. Will Book 3, page 287

2 cows and yearling, 1 dozen new spoons, 2 barren cows,1 young steer and heifer, 3 pas. forks and 6 of spire,

6 head of sheep, 2 towels,1 horse and mare, 2 pare of shears,25 new pewter, parcel of old iron, 42 old pewter, 1 chest and lumber,

parcel shoemakers' tools, chest and cane, parcel of books, chest and box, parcel of candle stubs, 2 mills bags. parcel of tin, 1 feather bed, and furn,

parcel of earthenware, parcel of glass bottles, parcel of old lumber, 2 lanterns, parcel of old spools, 2 bolts 2 spinning wheels parcel of segitt boots, collar and harness, parcel of small sillards, parcel of olifford, drinking glass, 2 parcel of lasts, looking glass, parcel of coopers and curing pans, and steel carpenters tools,

1 warming pan and sinior, 2 old pads, 3 pare of old wool cards, 4 new harness, pare of porbett comperios, 1 old chest and lumber, 1 gun and 1 rowing rod, parcel of nails,

parcel of bowels and trays, 4 old barrels, parcel of old chairs and 2 old mills bags
table and furniture, 2 bushels of soft joynte, 1 skillet, 1 linen wheel, 2 pare of fire tongs and 16 lb. wool, fire shovels, parcel of baskoft,1 spit, 2 saddles and bridles,

2 pots parcel of planks,1 cutting knife, parcel of banded leather, pare old baltol eddy hook, 1 brass cord, 2 raw hides parcel of old umblott old table, 2 shot bags and powder horns, 1 cart and wheels,

parcel of earthen ware, 1 hive of bees, copper pott old grinder, 2 frying pans, parcel of old carque, 1 spiro mortar, basrolls, 106 pott iron, parcel of cotton, 1 lines and harness, his own wearing clothes, 5 bushels of wheat, parcel of money, scales and rule, parcel of can hooks, 2/6 cash, 1 small auger, parcel of mall lumber, 6 years of caterloons, pare of large scales stuff, parcel of lumber.

Sarah Meador gave her son John Meador a yoke of oxen and a gun. Marks for these oxen were registered and marks for a black heifer were registered later for "John Meadors, son of Thomas Meadors of Hoskins Creek."

p.193: Swallow Forked on both ears overkeeled on the right ear pr pr marke of the cattle belonging to Susanna Meador daughter of Thomas Meador de cd cropt on the right ear and a slitt in the crop and underkeeled in same ear and a hole in the left ear is the ppr mark of the cattle belonging to Mary Meador daughter of Thomas Meador decd. A flower de Luce on the right ear and cropt on the left ear is the proper mark of cattle belonging to John Meador Son of Thomas Meador decd.

Cows were especially valuable since they had to be transported from England and were usually mentioned specifically in wills from this time, the killing of a cow was a capital crime.

A Devon cow, the breed most common in British Colonial America.

Whereas Abraham Coombe of the Province of Maryland Gent: did formerly put into the hands and possession of my late brother in law John Measor dec'd one heifer for the use and proper acco't of my Godson John Meader son of John Meader the Elder dec'd since w'ch the s'd John Meader the son dec'd in his minority. Now know all men by these presents that the s'd Abraham Coombe do by these p'sents give and grant unto Mary.

Advancement of Slavery in Virginia

The 1680s saw the consolidation of race-based slavery following Bacon's Rebellion in 1676. Wealthy planters, fearful of class conflict and reliant on their labor force, shifted from indentured servitude to permanent slavery for Africans.

Laws were enacted to make permanent servitude more explicitly linked to race, solidifying the societal and legal foundations of slavery.
The wealthy white landowners, or gentry, dominated the government and held significant power. Their control of the tobacco-based economy and

The landing of the first Negroes

Images showing the sale of Blacks as slaves, and of the link between tobacco and their servitude.

Thomas Meador Jr.
Sarah Hoskins

John Meador 1658–1721 • L89D-GTT	**Thomas Meador Jr** 1634–1662 • LJ58-5PJ	Thomas Meade Sr 1612–1655 • LTP4-TDF Marriage: 1635 England
Mary Francis Awbrey 1665–1721 • PST7-XDV	**Sarah Hoskins** 1637–1674 • M45Q-44R	Sarah Yates 1615–1655 • LCD7-CXG

Thomas Meador Jr., was born 1634 in Warrosquyoake, Virginia, British Colonial America. He was not yet of age when his father died in 1655. Hence the name Thomas, the Orphan. In August 1655 he petitioned the Court as an orphan to have William Underwood appointed his guardian. He died around April 13, 1662 in Old Rappahannock, Virginia, British Colonial America and was buried in Orphan Meador Cemetery Meade, Essex County, Virginia.

By 1634, by order of the King of England, Charles I, eight shires of Virginia were formed, with a total population of 4,914 settlers. Warrosquoake Shire included 522 persons at the time. It and Accomac Shire were the only shires given Native-American names, honoring the friendly tribes nearby.

In 1637, the English renamed it Isle of Wight County, after an island of the same name in the English Channel between England and France. They also renamed the Warrosquoake river the Pagan River. It was known as "Warrosquyoake Shire" until its 1637 renaming to "Isle of Wight County."

Warrosquyoake was an Algonquin-speaking tribe and a key area in the early British colonial period in Virginia. The tribe lived near the Pagan River and were part of the Powhatan Confederacy. Their main village was located on the Pagan River, near present-day Smithfield, Virginia.

A map of Virginia from the 1600's showing the James River and Pagan Creek.

"To all to whom these presents shall come, Greetings:....now know ye that I, the said Sir William Berkeley, Knight, Governor of Virginia, give and grant unto Thomas Meader, orphan, four hundred and fifty acres of land in Lancaster County on the South side of the head of Hoskins Creek, beginning at a poplar standing by the side of a Beaver Damnear the Indian Path and running South by West two hundred and fifty poles, thence parallel to the Dam West by North four hundred and fifty poles to the Dam to the first mentioned tree. The said land being first granted to Thomas Browning by patent dated the thirtieth of November, one thousand six hundred and fifty-seven, and by him assigned to John Cooke, and by him assigned to Thomas Meader deceased, and by his will given to the said Thomas Meader. To have and to hold [etc].

Sarah Hoskins was born around 1637 in York and died around 1674 in Rappahannock, Essex, Virginia, British Colonial America. She married Thomas, probably around 1658. Following Thomas' death, she married Henry Awbrey in around 1664. She is thought to have died around 1674, but that date is unclear.   Sarah is commonly considered to be Sarah Hoskins, said to be the daughter of Bartholomew. Hoskins but this relationship has been disputed.

The Grave of Sarah Hoskins Meador

The Will of Thomas Meads/Meador

The last will and testament of Tho. Meads (Meador) made the 5th. day of March (54.) Imp nt. I do bequeath my body to the Earth & my soul to God that gave it. I do make my wife my sole & absolute Excr. I do give to my wife and Daughter Mary this planation that I nowive upon and all the land on this side of the Creek, and the sd. plantation not to be my Daughter's 'till after my wife's decease.

I do give to my two sons Thos. & John Meads all the land that is on the west side of the Creek provided that they pay unto my two Daughters Margaret & Joyce out of the s. land two thousand pounds of tob. & cask at their day of marriage, and in case eithre of the(m) die that the sd. tob. to belong to the survivor.

I do give unto my wife & sons & my Daughters above mentioned all my goods and chattels after my debts are paid and that they shall be equally divided amongst them. I do give to my Daughter Anne all the cattle that belongeth to her which is about five head of cattle, and likewise I do give unto her one shilling in money.

This is my last will and testament as witness my hand the day & year above written. Sig: Thomas Mead. Witness: Rawleigh Travers, John Richardson, Edward Bradshaw (by his mark), pbat 6 da. Juny 1655.

Thomas Meador Jr	**Thomas Meade Sr**	William Meade, Sr.
1634–1662 • LJ58-5PJ	1612–1655 • LTP4-TDF	1587–Deceased • L5BP-959
	Marriage: 1635	Marriage: 1 November 1610
	England	Steeple Morden, Cambridgeshire, England
Sarah Hoskins	**Sarah Yates**	**Joane Deare**
1637–1674 • M45Q-44R	1615–1655 • LCD7-CXG	1592–1619 • GN83-ZJ8

One of the flags of Colonial Virginia

Thomas Meade, Sr.
Sarah Yates

First Meadors in British Colonial America
My 9th Great Great Grandfather

1612

Born December 24, 1612 in Suffolk England.

1636

He arrived by ship in Jamestown Colony on June 1, 1636, accompanied by his brother Ambrose. Unable to identify the ship or any passenger lists. There were less than 4,000 people in all of Virginia at that time. There were only eight counties of shires in the colonies. Jamestown was the first permanent English settlement in America, and had been founded 27 years earlier, in 1607.

The first documented record for Thomas Meades is a headright grant of 300 acres in 1636 to John Gater of Elizabeth City for the transportation of six men. One of those individuals was Thomas Meades. Based on the headright grant, Thomas came by himself, without a wife or children.

He married Sarah Yates in about 1637, a year after he emigrated. She was born around 1612 in Southwark, Christ Church, Surrey, England and was christened June 28th 1612 at Elland, Yorkshire, England. Her father was Isaac Yates. She died sometime after June 1655 in Lancaster, Virginia, British Colonial America.

Last Will and Testament of Thomas Meade Sr.
Dated 12 June 1655

Meade initially settled in Isle of Wight County, Virginia, and later moved around 1650 to the northeast shore of the Rappahannock River in what is now Richmond County. A general migration from the Isle of Wight to the northwest shore of the Rappahannock River (in present Richmond Co.) occurred about 1650, about the time the royal governor promoted an edict against the Puritan teachings.

1653

The records of Lancaster County, Virginia show that Thomas Meades purchased 700 acres from William Underwood on the northeast shore of the Rappahannock River between Milleck Creek and Bushwood Creek and first branch of what is today called Juggs Creek. This 700-acre purchase included more than a mile of choice river front property, including an excellent landing.

He built his home on high ground behind the river landing, between Juggs Creek and Balls Creek. Later the name "Islington" was attached to the grounds. Today, this land lies at the river end of Route 632 in Richmond County, Virginia, and the river landing is known as "Islington Landing."

1654

On 6 April 1654, he was appointed Constable, with the oath administered by James Williamson. He also receives 1000 acres for transport of 20 people, 7 Sept. 1654. He wrote his Will on 5 March 1655, and it was entered into probate on 6 June 1655.

1655

Died 6 June 1655, June 6, 1655 in Lancaster, Virginia, British Colonial America and buried in Thomas Orphan Meador Cemetery, Essex County, Virginia. He was survived by his wife, who was named as his executor, and six children.

Typical Supply Ship Supporting the Virginia Colony

The Last Will and Testament of Thomas Meads

"The last Will and Testament of Thomas Meads made the 5th. day of March (54.) Impnt. I do bequeath my body to the Earth & my soul to God that gave it. I do make my wife my sole & absolute Excr. I do give to my wife and Daughter Mary this plantation that I now live upon and all the land on this side of the Creek, and the sd. plantation not to be my Daughter's 'till after my wife's decease. I do give to my two sons Thos. & John Meads all the land that is on the west side of the Creek provided that they pay unto my two Daughters Margaret & Joyce out of the s. land two thousand pounds of tob. & cash at their day of marriage, and in case either of the[m] die that the sd. tob. to belong to the survivor. I do give unto my wife & sons & my Daughters above mentioned all my goods and chattels after my debts are paid and that they shall be equally divided amongst them. I do give to my Daughter Anne all the cattle that belongeth to her which is about five head of cattle, and likewise I do give unto her one shilling in money. This is my last will and testament as witness my hand the day & year above written."

Thomas Mead

Witness Rawleigh Travers, John Richardson Edward Bradshaw (by his mark)
pbat 6 da. Juny 1655".

Indigenous Peoples in the Virgina Colony

Indigenous peoples had been living in Virginia for over 12,000 years. The Powhatan Chiefdom inhabited the land around current Elizabeth City pre-1607 and was made up of over 30 tribes all ruled by the Powhatan paramount Chief. The Chiefdom controlled about 100 miles by 100 miles of land and had a population of about 25,000 people before the English arrived.

The river valley was occupied principally by the Rappahannock Indians, with a few villages of Mattaponi, Moratticoes, Totuskeys, Portobagoes, and others.

Shortly after the establishment of the Jamestown settlement in 1607, Capt. John Smith crossed the James River in search of food. He met the Warrosquyoake Indians who supplied him with several bushels of corn. Warrosquyoake was an Algonquin-speaking tribe and a key area in the early British colonial period in Virginia. The tribe lived near the Pagan River and were part of the Powhatan Confederacy.

In the winter of 1607, as a sign of peace, the chief of the Powhatan tribe sent gifts to settlements near Elizabeth City such as Jamestown often accompanied by his daughter Pocahontas.

In 1614, Pocahontas married the settler John Rolfe which aided peaceful relations between the Powhatans and settlers for a few years.

Relations deteriorated as English colonists encroached on Warrosquyoake land, leading to conflict known as the Indian Massacre of 1622 (as called by the settlers), or as the Powhatan Uprising. About 350-400 settlers were killed in the conflict, a large percent of the Virginia population of the time. Following the uprising, the Warrosquyoake tribe gradually disappeared from colonial records. The land was later formalized as Warrosquyoake Shire in 1634 and renamed Isle of Wight County in 1637.

Original drawing of a Powhotan Native American

White settlement was initially forbidden above the Pamunkey River; later this prohibition was only for the land above the Piscattaway and Totuskey Creeks. But many settlers filed claims upon the choice river front lands, and by 1646-1650 grants were being given along the Rappahannock River. The tribes who called this land home were forced into the forested lands behind the mile-deep grants. William Underwood. and James Williamson both received grants in this area. Both sold portions of their grants to the Meadors.

In November 1654, in The Virginia Assembly used complaints against the Rappahannock Indians to justify raising a militia in three counties: Lancaster 100 men, Northumberland 40 and Westmoreland 30, to meet on the first Wednesday in February.

As a reflection of Thomas' standing in the community, his plantation was chosen as a rallying point for this army. The excellent landing at the plantation and the proximity of the Indian village also had bearing on the choice of Thomas' land, which was near the present town of Warsaw. The army marched from Thomas' grounds, overland to the village of the Rappahannock Indians. The purpose of their visit was to ensure peace, without provoking hostilities.

In 1661, an Indian raid took place on the neighboring plantation of Richard White. Thomas White and two other men were brutally murdered. Perhaps as many as 300 people were killed in multiple Indian raids. Demanding protection, the settlers petitioned the Jamestown Government for arms, forts and soldiers.

A Map of Jamestown from 1606 as described by Captain John Smith, showing the location of Native American tribes nearby.

William Harold Meadows, Sr.
Dad

Harriett Aline Cole Meadows
Mother

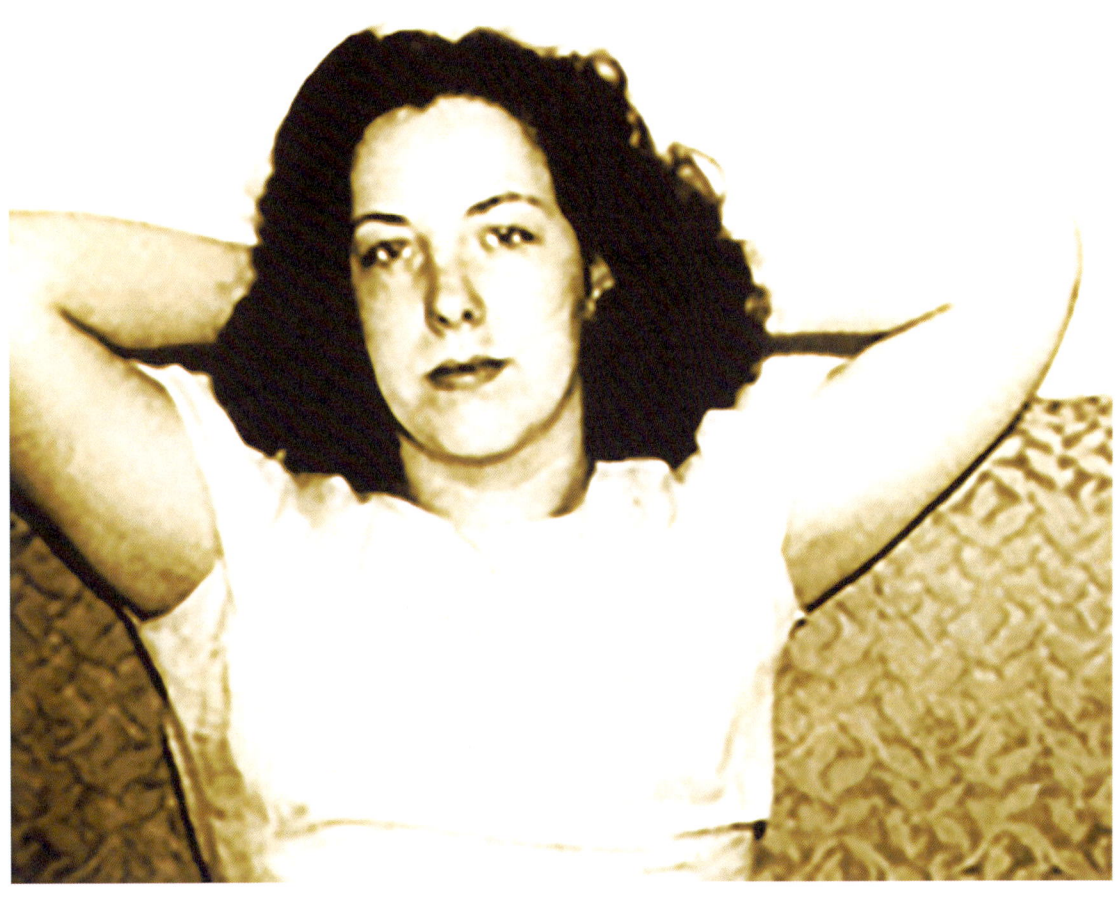

www.ingramcontent.com/pod-product-compliance
Lightning Source LLC
LaVergne TN
LVRC100725070526
838199LV00020B/547